A CONSERVATIVE ALTERNATIVE SCHOOL: THE A+ SCHOOL IN CUPERTINO

By William M. Pursell

Library of Congress Catalog Card Number: 75-39098
ISBN 0-87367-067-1
Copyright © 1976 by The Phi Delta Kappa Educational Foundation
Bloomington, Indiana

TABLE OF CONTENTS

Introduction 7

Background 8
   Cupertino 9
   Time to Experiment 10
   Goals of the District 11
   "Something for Everyone" 12

Proposal for a Pilot Program 14
   1. Statement of Purpose 14
   2. Philosophy/Principles and Attitudes 14
   3. Goals, Aims, and Objectives 17
   4. Means of Attaining Aims 18

Developing Interest in the Program 21
   An Open Meeting for Parents 21
   Road Blocks 23
   Naming the Program 24
   Language in the Flier 24
   Developing a Curriculum 25
   Finding Schools for the Program 27
   Problems After the Year Started 29
   How We Tried to Expand 31

How A+ Differs from the "Regular Program" 33
   Field Trips 33
   Homework 34
   Dress Code 34
   Discipline 35
   Method of Instruction 35
   Report Cards 36
   Successes of the Program 37
   Pressures Against the Program 37

Conclusions 39

INTRODUCTION

This fastback, written by a parent with deep concerns and active involvement in his school district, has two major themes. One is the rationale for a conservative alternative school. The other is the record of his untiring efforts to have such a school introduced in Cupertino.

These two issues, the values of a traditional curriculum and the problems of instituting change in a school program, are both universal and are of potential interest to all teachers, parents, administrators, and others genuinely concerned with providing the most appropriate educational opportunities for all children. The difficulties encountered in the process of getting this program established are important reminders of the kinds of problems associated with achieving change in any school district.

BACKGROUND

Would your school system get a 98 percent favorable response if you asked the question, "Are you satisfied with your school this year?"

In January, 1975, we asked the parents of the youngsters in our school, "Are you satisfied with the Academics-Plus Program at your child's school this year?" Ninety-eight percent responded "Yes."

In that "yes" vote lies, perhaps, the key to parent satisfaction of the middle-class family. This group has been the backbone of the public school system in America. If they are not kept satisfied, the public school system is indeed in trouble, because the group will no longer support it.

What is it that brought this satisfaction?

To many, Academics-Plus is nothing more than their school pretty much as they know it and see it every day; basic subjects taught to elementary school children in a somewhat structured classroom environment with standard textbooks, according to a standard curriculum, by a good teacher. Teaching methods and materials have good continuity from one year to the next. Bright kids and not so bright kids are in the same classroom. Differing reading groups, math groups, science groups, and so on are within most classrooms so that children can work at the speeds that suit them best. Teachers have the support of parents and principal. Standardized evaluative testing and written report cards fairly and accurately report progress against a set of standards and against class average. In short, it is school as most of us knew it when we were children in schools all over the country.

What makes it unique today is that we, the parents, have created a program in which we no longer take potluck in the selection of teachers and teaching methods from year to year. Parents' desires for their children's education are matched with the type of classroom which will provide it. Standards of home and school are similar. There is free choice to enroll in this program, to have it instead of being forced into it or into something else. The emphases are on the cognitive domain, on the facts the child needs to know for continuing education, and on a sense of achievement throughout his life.

If this is pretty close to what you have in your school, for heaven's sake don't lose it.

Cupertino

Many people in the Cupertino Union School District are shocked to find that this small program is labeled an alternative program. "Isn't this what our kids have at our school now?" is the most frequently asked question when they find out about us.

To be labeled an "alternative" implies that one program or idea differs from the regular offering. The story of the Academics-Plus Program is the story of that difference. Let us tell you a little of its background.

The Cupertino Union School District covers thirty-six elementary and six junior high schools in all or part of six cities and towns at the southern end of San Francisco Bay. It grew to this size in approximately seven years (1957-64) from an original four elementary schools nestled in among thousands of acres of apricot and cherry trees, and is now the largest elementary district in California.

During its growth period, a time in which the population of its area grew from perhaps 4,000 or 5,000 to nearly 200,000 people, the district built a reputation as one of the finest districts in California.

Because of the sudden emergence of the space and missile industry, the electronics industry, and the computer industry, a tremendous migration of engineers, technologists, and middle management flooded the area. They brought good income, high socioeconomic levels, intelligence, and few problems, except the problem of too many people too quickly.

Schools were added at a rate of six or seven a year, and good teachers were recruited with high salaries. Many who came as teachers became principals in a short time. Quite a few of the latter group did well in that category also, but not all. A few became living proof of the principle that some people rise to their own level of incompetence.

Time to Experiment

About ten years ago, things began to change.

Educators who had been working at fever pitch to get classrooms built as fast as the subdivisions which were to fill them suddenly found themselves with time on their hands. Time to "innovate." Time to experiment. New ideas needed to be played with—new philosophies, new techniques, new teaching methods. Some were good, some were not; some made students, some made anarchists. But few, if any, of the bad ones were ever dropped.

But educators weren't the only ones to blame for the changes. Parents had become very divided over what they expected from education. One group expected the schools to teach the basics as they, the parents, had learned them: the three R's, history, spelling, art, P.E., etc. A second group expected something very different from the schools. This group didn't care about basics; they wanted their children to learn to enjoy life, to be happy, to be well adjusted, to love, and so on. Reading and writing would come in time when the children were ready. A third group of parents seemed to have no goals for their children and didn't seem to know or care what was going to happen to them.

The last two groups of parents played nicely into the hands of those educators who needed recognition and who got it through innovation, experimentation, and publication. More and more programs and innovative ideas were brought forth, sounding good to some people, but resulting in great dissatisfaction to others. Test scores dropped in several of the basic skills areas. Some parents found their family's values openly challenged in the classroom and their children's attitudes being molded and reshaped in directions counter to the wishes of the parents. Some people were greatly displeased, and many of those who could afford it began pulling their children out of the public schools and putting them into private and parochial schools.

The general trend of the innovative ideas and programs was toward "open classrooms," "individualized instruction," "differentiated staffing," "behavior modification," "educating the whole child," etc. While not all of these ideas are wholly bad, their implementation by incompletely trained people on children whose parents were not in favor of the ideas in the first place left many parents extremely frustrated and angry. Too often, also, the failures of teachers were blamed on the parents or children or both. "Open classroom" can mean anything from a highly structured operation with a very fine teacher and program and excellent results to a mindless being who sits cross-legged on the floor, who calls itself a "facilitator," who has no curriculum or program, and who leaves thirty children bored, ignorant, and frustrated for a whole school year.

Goals of the District

The goals of the district were a "wishy-washy" set of generalities with no objectives attached, no specifics, no real purpose. There was no reward for success and no penalty for failure for students, teachers, or administrators.

The district instituted a management philosophy of "participatory democracy" which meant that each of the forty-two schools was almost completely autonomous in most areas. The superintendent and the board lost (or gave away) much of their authority to the local school and its teachers and so diffused the responsibility for what went on that any sense of central control over the programs of the local school was lost.

A standard curriculum was a thing of the past. In its place was a very general "recommended" curriculum put out, with no power of insistence upon its use, by the county superintendent's office. Two copies of it were available at every school, but few teachers ever looked at it, which was probably just as well. Its emphasis was very heavy in art and music, and it mentioned English only as a second language and only briefly.

With neither a curriculum nor much central control over what went on, things verged near chaos in some schools. Every teacher did her own thing. Some children were taught reading by as many as four different teaching methods in the first three years. One can readily imagine the results. Children were passed on from teacher to teacher, from year to year, without anyone worrying about whether anything had been learned, or what it was, or by what method, or how well. All students passed because they were a year older, and the teachers got their step in class raises for being in the system a year longer (and more if they took another unit of education courses during the year).

Parents were told their children were progressing satisfactorily. Many didn't wake up to reality until they moved to another district, where many children were "put back," or until the child reached high school, where as many as 31 percent were required to take remedial reading or math in the ninth grade because they lacked the preparation for high school work. When they awoke it was too late for the child. Years of his life and his preparation for the rest of his life were wasted. Habit patterns of learning and working were missed or mistrained.

Small groups and large groups of parents were complaining. They were upset. Their children were not learning to read, to spell, to punctuate. Their views of history and economics were being distorted. They did not want the school personnel messing in the very gray areas of the child's psyche. How can a youngster "feel good about himself" if he is ignorant?

It was against this background that two of us decided to run for two of the three seats open in the 1973 school board election. After a particularly hard-fought campaign, we were ultimately defeated by a narrow margin. During the campaign we heard horror story after horror story from unhappy parents.

On the morning after our defeat, April 17, someone said to us, "You know, we have never spelled out what it is we want. All we have been doing for years has been reacting to what they are doing to us." After giving that some thought, we decided perhaps it was time we told the board and administration what it was we wanted.

"Something for Everyone"

Our opponents in the campaign had run on a platform of something for everyone. We would never have a better opportunity than now to let them prove they meant it. One of our opponents had, the year before, been successful in getting the board to approve an Open Kindergarten Program ("OK") at one of the schools. She recently had it extended to include the primary grades, and it was carried as an "alternative program" by the district.

We decided to take her original proposal and reword it to fit what we wanted as a program for our children. Its original wording was a sweetly open approach, but its form was good, and it had been successful in getting board approval. After one quiet Sunday morning we had a reworked version to use as a proposal from which to bargain.

After the rough draft proposal had been prepared, a group of nearly thirty people who had worked on our campaign met and agreed, generally, on the wording of the final draft. But it was also generally agreed that the group was too large for effective committee work. So a smaller committee of about ten very interested people was selected to push the project. The steering committee was born.

PROPOSAL FOR A PILOT PROGRAM

Our original proposal read as follows:

May 17, 1973
Proposal for a Pilot Program—
Cupertino Union School District

1. Statement of Purpose

We propose the establishment of a pilot program within the Cupertino Union School District 1) beginning with one class of each grade in each K-6 school in September, 1973; 2) including a basic curriculum; 3) operating on a formal basis in method and structure; and 4) involving parents as participants in the selection of teachers and principals and in the planning and execution of the program.

2. Philosophy—Principles and Attitudes

We believe that the primary duty of the public schools should be to prepare children for a productive life as responsible citizens in a free and competitive society, and to give them the basic tools they will need to continue to learn. We believe this will be accomplished by:

——teaching them to read, write, speak, spell, and compute accurately and effectively, to know and understand our history, heritage, and governmental structure, and to reason in a logical and objective manner. Competence in these fundamentals must be achieved at the earliest grades possible to allow time for expansion of these subjects and others now considered enrichment.

——challenging each child to do his best by requiring that his work be done properly and on time, and corrected so that his final exposure to each subject area be one of success and satisfaction.

——reinforcing parental teachings of citizenship, discipline, respect, and personal responsibility.

——reporting to parents accurately and comprehensively, in writing, the child's progress against a measurable set of standards (academic performance objectives) and against the class average.

——teaching all sides of controversial issues fairly and completely.

——eliminating group labeling and stereotyping.

We believe that some children:

——learn best in a structured environment.

——are happiest when they can see measurable progress in themselves.

——need the thrill of competition with one another and against measurable standards.

——need to learn to overcome frustration and occasional defeats and to grow successfully from their frustrations and defeats.

——are capable of learning more and at a more rapid rate than others and should be given the opportunity to do so.

——are easily distracted by unstructured classrooms in which people move in various directions and are involved in a wide variety of simultaneous activities.

——have better natural learning experiences in a structured classroom with a good teacher.

We believe that parents:

——should not have to put their children into private or parochial schools to give them a basic academic education of high quality and standards.

——have the right to expect that their children will not be made the subjects of experimentation without their consent.

——have the right to expect that the public schools will give their children a firm grounding in fundamental subjects upon which the students can build the rest of their lives.

——differ as to what they want their children to learn in the public schools, but that a significant number wish their children to receive a higher level of preparation in the basics than is currently being offered in the district. (They are more concerned that their children be given this preparation than that an inordinate amount of school time be spent on becoming "well adjusted" or "getting along with others.") Some parents would prefer that their children learn to be independent rather than interdependent.

——have the right to expect that their children will not need to have the progress of their education interrupted in high school by being required to take remedial math or reading. We believe that proven and realistic teaching methods will preclude this type of remedial work.

——have the right to live their own lives secure in the knowledge that the public schools, to which they have entrusted their children's education, and for which they are paying through taxes, will do a satisfactory job of imparting that education without the direct involvement of the parent being needed as a "watchdog" or as an "assistant to the teacher."

——have the right to expect that the reporting system used by the school and the teacher gives them an accurate, complete, and factual measurement of their child's progress against a measurable set of standards, including letter grades.

We believe that learning:

——can be accomplished in a structured classroom, and that this type of classroom need not be antithetical to the development of a "positive self-concept" or "self-esteem." Expected standards and schedules are consonant with a child's sense of security, which is a vital part of the development of a good self-image.

——must be accomplished, if children are to assume a productive place in a modern world, and can best be accomplished in an orderly and organized atmosphere.

We believe that an atmosphere:

——which is warm and friendly, but which provides a structured and positive approach to the business at hand, is most conducive to learning for our children.

——which is constantly challenging to a child's desire to excel and to learn becomes exciting, interesting, and conducive to success in school.

We believe that schools:

——have the right to institute a reasonable code of dress, deportment, and discipline. (We feel that there is a direct correlation between inappropriate dress appearance and a student's general work habits, self-esteem, and attitude toward learning.)

——should make these rules known to children and parents.

3. Goals, Aims, and Objectives

We desire that our children gain a firm grounding in basic

subjects and enrichment areas at the earliest time possible in the elementary school so that their opportunities for further learning in high school and college are enhanced.

Areas we wish included in the curriculum would include, at appropriate levels: reading, writing, spelling, speech, composition, grammar, arithmetic through fractions and decimals and beginning algebra, history, geography, government and economics, art, music, drama, physical education, physical fitness, science (physical, biological, and ecological), library use and research skills, and other subjects which may, from time to time, be considered beneficial to the children by teachers and parents.

4. Means of Attaining Aims

A. Staff:
   1. Principals—We believe that the principal can have a profound effect on the success of the program. We would like principals who have a sincere belief in this style of education, who could work together with us and the teachers to attain our common goals. We would expect him to be fair, honest, and friendly, while affording firm and consistent leadership for teachers and students alike. We desire that he lend his support, interest, and encouragement on the basis of honest communication.
   2. Teachers—We would like to have teachers who would personally desire to teach in this type of classroom. We expect and welcome full participation of teachers in curriculum planning. Such teachers should be capable of commanding respect and attention from students by their ability and warmth, rather than by fear or force. We would expect them to be people whom the children can admire and look up to with respect because of the positive example they set for them in attitude, ability, and deportment. We would

welcome teachers of various ethnic and cultural backgrounds who could impart to the children a respect for peoples of various cultures and backgrounds on a natural and reasonable basis.

3. Coordinating Committee—This committee, consisting of parents and teachers involved in the program, should be established at the beginning of the program. The purpose is to establish and provide a continuity of implementation and assessment of the curriculum.

4. Parents—Parents should be available upon request of the teacher for consultation and as resource persons. They should be expected to back the faculty in any extracurricular activities within reasonable scope of the curriculum. They should not, however, be expected to be involved in the classroom teaching on a regular basis.

B. Facilities:
   1. Schools—We would like to have one class of each grade in each K-6 school devoted to this program.
   2. Equipment—Only the normal school equipment which other schools have.
   3. Program—We would expect to operate on the same school calendar and on the same daily schedule as the rest of the district. We would expect the same pupil-teacher ratio as the rest of the district. We will expect to comply with all requirements of the State Education Code. Because some children may initially need help to catch up to the curriculum goals for their particular grade, we may need the assistance of reading and math specialists in the initial months of this program. This determination, and requests for assistance, should be made by the teacher and the principal. In cases where a child cannot do the

work for the grade level, the decision on his grade placement should be jointly made by teacher, principal, and parents. The concept of social promotion because of chronological age only should be carefully and individually evaluated.

C. Operating Procedure:
1. Enrollment—Students would be enrolled on a first come, first served basis in each attendance area.
2. Transportation—Normal school bus transportation or walking, unless the program, for some reason, is not available at the home school. Parents would then have to assume responsibility.

D. Evaluation:

We would like to have each grade level evaluated by Stanford Achievement Tests or other appropriate standardized tests at regular intervals three times a year to determine progress of students against academic performance objectives. Results of these tests should be reported to the school board and to parents immediately and would serve as the basis on which written report cards are made out for each student. We would expect comparative evaluation with any other school in the district of comparable I.Q. ability students.

E. Communication of Availability of Program:

We request that the school district circulate notice of the availability of this program immediately, so that all parents may have the opportunity to participate in development of the program at their school.

DEVELOPING INTEREST IN THE PROGRAM

With this proposal we asked for and got a meeting with the superintendent and his assistants on May 14, 1973. We delivered copies to them in advance so that they did not come to the meeting unprepared. Their immediate reaction to the proposal was that what we were requesting was little different from the "regular" program of the district. But they recognized that there were differences and that it should be brought to the board at the next regular meeting.

The board, still filled with the old members, approved the idea after very brief discussion and gave the administration the approval needed to proceed.

An Open Meeting for Parents

The next step was to determine whether parents were interested in sufficient numbers to establish the program. The superintendent sent out a notice on June 1, 1973, for an open meeting on June 6 for parents to come and indicate their interest.

A meeting with one of the associate superintendents was held to plan for the open meeting. It was important that such a meeting not be allowed to get out of hand and degenerate into a chronicle of the angers and frustrations of those attending the meetings, either from the podium or from the audience. So we all had our parts of the program rehearsed.

June 6 arrived as the hottest day on record in the Santa Clara Valley. By 7:30 p.m. the temperature was still well over

100 degrees. The administration had planned for a meeting of about 100 people, "probably no more than 125 people." By 7:30 more than 300 people were packed into an un-air-conditioned room. For the most part, they didn't try to tell about the awful situations at their schools. They just listened with a restrained desperation. When it was over, almost all signed up to participate in the program.

We really didn't have much to offer them at this meeting or in a few subsequent weeks—just an idea of what we wanted, but without a knowledge of where the program would be, what the curriculum would look like, what sort of teachers or principals we could get, what transportation problems we would encounter, etc. They signed up anyway. At least they were interested in it, but there was a solid need to get facts for them as quickly as possible. Our phones began to ring immediately after the meeting and, so far, we had little concrete information to give those who were calling.

It was decided by the committee and the associate superintendent appointed to work with us that we had to have some indication of which school areas had the heaviest potential enrollment. It would be in these school areas that we would try to start the program if we couldn't get it started in every school in the district for the first year—and we knew we did not have a prayer of that.

A succession of meetings were held in late June with the associate superintendent and the committee to refine the details of what we wanted in the program and what we wanted to say and could say in an interest indicator flier.

Very early in this phase of our work the district personnel began to take a very defensive posture toward us and what we were doing. As long as our wording was both nonspecific and noncomparative we represented little threat. But the minute we became specific and started to make comparisons to program or methods, or to use comparative words such as "more" or "greater," we encountered increasing hostility and defensiveness. It was understandable. The district was proud of what it was doing or thought it was doing. We were regarded as renegades and as a threat to the status quo and to all the "neat" programs and innovative things they were trying.

Road Blocks

It was soon apparent to the committee that if we were to be ready to have a program in the fall we were going to have to get a great many things together quickly. It was also apparent that road blocks were being dropped in our way from somewhere. We heard objections to wording, hints that just too much had to be done before fall, that teachers and principals were lacking, and so on.

The old board was now out of office, and the new board (the three who had opposed us) was newly installed. Perhaps a source of help for the removal of road blocks existed there.

We decided to ask to be heard under "delegations" at the next board meeting to update the new board on our plans. We didn't tell the administration that what we wanted from the board were some clear indications of the board's intentions toward seeing our program succeed. I am not sure how far any of the committee had really thought out the possibilities of such a confrontation, but the meeting went well for us.

We reported on our progress to date. As of July 3, 1973, we had more than 400 potential enrollees if we could make the program go. But we were facing an increasing opposition of a very shadowy nature. Could the board help with some direction?

The three new members, anxious to verify their commitment to something for everyone, and unaware that no action was supposed to be taken on any item brought up under delegations, proceeded to give the direction we needed. The administration was to see to it that our program was to be ready by September, 1973. They concluded, as we had, that our best chance for success lay in planning to start in three schools where the parental interest was the highest and that we should try for one class in each of the six grades in these schools. They agreed that an informational pre-enrollment form should be sent out to parents. They limited sending it, however, to parents of 10,000 summer school students rather than parents of all 22,000 students in the district.

We got the boost we needed. The two other members of the board were firmly committed to our program already, and the decisions were 5 to 0 in our favor.

Naming the Program

At about this time the administration suggested that we needed a name to identify us. After much discussion and numerous suggestions, the name Academics Plus was agreed upon, with the abbreviation of A+ to be used when we wanted it. This has come back to haunt us in two respects and should be approached with caution by anyone setting up a similar program. We wanted a name which would imply that the academics subject areas would be stressed but that at the same time, there would be room for other subjects such as art, music, physical education, etc. However, the A+ contraction produced the myth that the program was only for students of superior intellect and outstanding accomplishment. The district already had a very active, heavily funded Extended Learning Program (ELP) for this type of child. At the state level this program is labeled Mentally Gifted Minors (MGM). This program is a wonderful ego trip for the parents of the child with the identified high I.Q., but has the drawback of removing the bright child from children of varied I.Q. levels and family backgrounds and putting him into an ivory tower environment with a high snob potential. This can hurt the classroom he leaves by removing his mental stimulation from the rest of the children and can foster in him an elitist complex that may take years of hard knocks to remove.

Our problem is one of educating parents to understand that we want to unite, in one classroom, the bright, the average, and the below-average learner into a heterogeneous grouping of youngsters. This is the way he is going to find most people for the rest of his life. He may pick his friends from among one class, but he will be thrown together with other classes in work, in recreational activities, in civic and fraternal groups, and so on. In each such group he can learn something from the others, just as they can learn something from him. To us it is the essence of a democratic system, but our A+ name suggests the opposite to many.

Language in the Flier

In late June and early July, 1973, we were caught on the horns of a dilemma. In a preliminary draft of the flier to be sent to all parents of children enrolled in summer school in the district to determine potential enrollment, we had some words and phrases such as "greater emphasis on the fundamentals" and "more structured classroom environment than the regular district program." The administration wanted these phrases eliminated and wanted "no odious comparisons" made to the regular district program. This was understandable, and we recognized that if we were going to get the district to send out the mailing we had to change it. We tried to remove the comparative words and to redefine and restate our program in a variety of ways, none of which suited them. This exercise consumed several meetings of our steering committee with the associate superintendent, but still they objected. Finally, in desperation, one of us asked the question we should have asked weeks before, "We've defined our wants and needs as carefully as we can. We've tried to remove comparisons. You keep telling us we are not sufficiently different from the regular district program. Well then, what *is* the regular district program?"

They were stumped! They did not know. They thought they had a pretty good idea of what it was, but without a curriculum, without any real evaluation, and without getting out of their offices to go see what was happening in the classroom, they really didn't know what the "regular district program" was. The fact is that there was none.

Most of our original wording was restored, and in a few minutes we had a sign-up flier for distribution. It went out on July 16 to the parents of approximately 10,000 children enrolled in summer school. Within a week we had more than 800 children signed up. By the end of August it was more than 1,000.

Developing a Curriculum

The absence of a "regular program" made necessary the development of a curriculum for the program. After several fumbling attempts, we recruited the assistance of a retired teacher, three teachers from the Cupertino Teacher's Association, three teachers who wanted to teach in the program, and three former teachers who, as parents, were members of the steering committee. Within two weeks they had a curriculum which insured coverage of all the necessary subject areas, with the exception of an active physical education and calisthenics program. It provided for good articulation from one year to the next without skipping areas and without boring the children with undue repetition of subjects covered the previous year. It provided an opportunity to master basic subjects—the three R's, history, sciences, and social studies, and allowed room for art, music, health education, and other areas which make for a well-rounded youngster. Physical education was listed in the curriculum but without a calisthenics program, and active physical education happened more through recess games than through a planned active program.

The absence of a curriculum plan for the "regular program" of the district seems to be based on the desire to allow the teacher to be flexible in the teaching of subject matter. This is all very well, but it leaves a tremendous gap in the learning of some children. It also leads to some very real problems when children go from one grade to the next and to a very bad situation when the children leave the eighth grade and enter high school in a separate district and separate political entity. As mentioned before, more than 31 percent of the graduates from some of our junior high schools were (and are) being required to take remedial math and English classes in the ninth grade to meet high school standards. Part of the problem was a lack of communication between the elementary district and the high school district on what would be needed for the high school. This resulted in some students arriving totally unprepared in certain subject areas, and in others arriving at high school having finished material in junior high which they would get again in the ninth grade. The underprepared student (and his parents) ended up very frustrated because they thought the youngster was doing grade level work and his report cards had given them this assurance. The student who must repeat work successfully completed in junior high feels it is all a big waste of time—and it is!

Real communication seems to be lacking equally between teachers of various grades within the district on what a given student has had in the previous grade. Each teacher is doing her own thing. They may exchange information in the teacher's lounge, but apparently a real attempt to find and fill the gaps in a specific youngster's learning seldom occurs. In the attempt to avoid regimentation of teachers and pupils through a standardized curriculum, the district has created a disorganization bordering on a rout. The solution will require some giving on both sides but must ultimately result in some form of standardization of curriculum and teaching methods both in the K-8 grades and with the high school district.

Finding Schools for the Program

Simultaneously with the development of the curriculum, the steering committee was busy receiving and tallying the enrollment forms as they came in. Three schools had been designated to have first through sixth grade A+ classes.

By the first of August three schools had received the largest sign-up from the flier sent out to summer school parents. These were also the three with the greatest number of empty classrooms in which the classes might be placed. More than 300 youngsters were involved in the three schools. The remaining 700 applicants were scattered among the other thirty-nine schools in the district, and none had enough in any one grade level (thirty) to establish a class. The administration announced that the three schools would have A+ classes.

The board had specified that no additional funding was available to help A+. No substandard-sized classes would be approved; we had to have thirty children in each class. We were in a dilemma.

At about this time the principal at one school announced his resignation to take a job in another district. As his replacement, a man was brought in from another district. After he arrived he learned that he was to have one of the A+ schools and he also found out how set against A+ his teachers were. He was not willing to try setting up the program in such a hostile environment, and many parents who had indicated a desire for A+ were willing to back down when told they would get structured teaching but without the label.

At another school not enough students were enrolled to establish classes of thirty unless some students came from other schools, or unless we agreed to combination classes, or unless some other parents could be counselled to enroll their children in the program. The staff was hostile to the idea of A+, and the principal, with only two years to go to retirement, was reluctant to rock the boat. We began to get reports of parents being counselled out of the program. Their youngsters would be given structured teaching without the label, we heard.

We began a telephone campaign to try to determine which parents from the other thirty-nine schools would be willing to transport their children from their home school to one of these two schools. Results were disappointing. Most parents would not or could not undertake the daily transporting of their youngsters. We tried to arrange car pools with almost the same results. We watched our numbers fall away as September approached, and we died a little with each dropout. We heard more and more reports of other principals counselling their parents against sending their children away from the home school. Their motive was that they couldn't stand the loss of their A.D.A. (average daily attendance—the figure on which their school's share of state revenues was based). But we began to get more and more reports from parents that they had been told we were crackpots or that our program would be psychologically damaging to their children.

The third school was different. Here the principal told us frankly that he favored the more open approach, but that if the parents wanted A+ he would see that they got it to the very best of his ability. And he did! He selected six teachers who were using the structured approach, went over the suggested curriculum with them and sold it, counselled enough parents into the program to fill the classes after those of us from other schools had indicated our willingness to transfer in and transport our children. He kept up the counselling until classes were filled. He helped us sell the teachers on the need for a letter grade report card which accurately evaluated the pupil's achievement. He became known derisively to some of his associates as "Mr. A+".

His problems became compounded when, on the opening day of school, the district was hit by a teacher strike. The principal issue was more pay, but there were other issues. About two-thirds of the teachers were out for four days. Despite the bitterness and name calling, which may take some years to live down, school started with about 175 children in A+.

Each family is given a brief handbook on the Academics-

Plus Program which lays out the program as their children will find it. It expects and demands the parents' cooperation. The program and the school have received excellent support from parents, primarily because the results have been good.

Problems After the Year Started

We had a little problem with a few children who had been discipline problems in their previous school, and we had several who had been diagnosed as severely mentally handicapped. We became concerned that A+ was becoming a dumping ground. But soon the problems began to straighten themselves out. The discipline problems found they were not going to "get away with that stuff" at this school. If the teacher sent him to the principal, it was not to play checkers with him, as it had been at their previous school. The children with the handicaps turned out, in all but one case, simply to have been terrified by an unstructured class of ninety to 120 pupils and three or four teachers and five or six aides. They learned under the gentle but firm guidance of a single teacher in a class of thirty and came out of their shells.

Our request for standardized testing three times a year was cut to twice a year because of costs and an overcrowded computer. Originally it had been intended to provide the teacher with a standardized assessment of what the child knew at the beginning of the year so she could place emphasis where it was needed. The second testing would come approximately midyear to provide the teacher and parents with an assessment of how the child was progressing. The third testing would come just before the end of the year to determine whether the child had progressed sufficiently to go on to the next grade.

For a variety of reasons, the first test was not given until the end of October, and the results of that test were not made available to teachers until the first week in April. It took pressure from board members on the administrator responsible for testing to get the results then. By that time the results were useless to assist the teachers classifying students. But the test administered at the end of May showed that the children were learning well—at nearly twice the national norm.

At the beginning of the school year, Academics-Plus students were equivalent to the national norms in math, three months above national norms in reading, and one month below in language arts. By the end of the school year, Academics-Plus students were above national norms in all three subject areas—a year in reading, four months in language arts, and six months in math. The A+ intermediate grades showed greater growth across the three SRA subtests than did the primary grades. The total Academics-Plus Program generally scored at or above district norms on reading and math and below district norms on language arts.

Almost immediately after the start of school we began to get exciting reports from some parents of youngsters in the program. They could see progress in their children at home as well as in their school homework. Relationships with brothers and sisters were better, and the youngsters' attitude toward school was more positive. Several members of the committee could see similar results in their own children. In early January, 1974, we sent home a questionnaire to all parents asking their attitudes toward the program after four months of operation. The results were far better than we had hoped. More than 85 percent of the replies were highly favorable.

Eighty-five percent or more of the parents said their child's attitude was better at home, in the neighborhood, and toward school. When asked to give the school a report card on their child's progress compared to past years, more than 60 percent thought the writing, spelling, and arithmetic had improved better than previously. Fifty percent or more thought reading, English, history, geography, and citizenship had improved better than previously. In each category, no more than 5 percent of the parents thought the progress wasn't as good as it had been in past years. Ninety-three percent of the parents said they preferred report cards that included ABCDF grades, and 94 percent were satisfied with the discipline maintained.

We decided to give the school board another progress report on the basis of the parent evaluation. After telling the board what we were doing and how the program was working, we had several parents tell how it had affected their children and two of the teachers relate their feelings about teaching in the program. We were also able to insert a reminder that fewer than one-fifth of those who had indicated a desire to participate had been accommodated in the program.

How We Tried to Expand

We asked the board for the opportunity to try again to expand the program in the fall. Permission was granted for two more schools, and we started once more to try to fill eighteen classes in three schools. This would be only 540 children. More than a thousand had signed up originally.

Again we prepared sign-up sheets. We revised those used before and added material to inform prospective parents of results during part of the first year. On February 4, 1974, we took our parent and teacher representatives to a meeting of principals and had them tell their story again. Here we were received politely but unenthusiastically. The same problem, a potential loss of A.D.A. if children left their schools, was apparent to all. And none was brave enough to volunteer his school or his teachers to be one of the three schools. We had hoped they would volunteer, but when we left we knew we would have to battle it out again. Even the statements of our teachers, that it was exciting to be able to teach in the manner they felt most comfortable and to have the full backing of the parents, didn't sway the principals. No one was going to stick his neck out.

So the administration again selected the same three schools. Two were having severe problems with parent dissatisfaction. This time, however, the principal at one promised he would help counsel children into the program and he did. We were able to get a sixth-grade class established there in the fall of 1974.

The remaining school was another story. Here the principal was completely opposed to our philosophy and, with a small group of parents backing him, published a proposal for semistructured "A+-like" classes for parents who wanted them. With the proposal that he sent out to parents who indicated a desire for A+ he also sent a letter indicating that an outside group was trying to take over their school and would eliminate the parents' right to determine how and what their children would be taught. His proposal used most of the material we had written and promised most of what was being delivered in the A+ Program. It had the desired effect of cutting the numbers of those requesting the A+ Program. Part of the blame for the disappointment belongs to the parents, who have consistently refused to transport their children even when the steering committee has tried to work out car pooling arrangements. They complain about how their children are not learning but will not exercise their rights if it means driving across town to put their youngsters in a successful program.

HOW A+ DIFFERS FROM THE "REGULAR PROGRAM"

So where are we now? What do we have in our six classes in one school and one class in another school? How do we differ from the "regular program" of the district?

The classes now average twenty-seven students in the first, second, and third grades and thirty in the fourth, fifth, and sixth grades. Each grade has a self-contained classroom with children grouped for learning according to ability levels within the class and according to the teaching qualifications and talents of the teachers. Some teachers have found that they can do a more thorough job of teaching by sending a few of their students into another teacher's class for math or science or music for a period during the school day. Each teacher can then concentrate on a group at one level as their needs develop. But the basic composition of the class is of a heterogeneous group of children working in the classroom together, and many are finding they can learn a great deal from each other.

The teacher determines what the children will be taught and when and how. Except in rare instances the teacher makes the decisions. She may allow the class to feel that it is making some decisions if she wishes, but she, not the class, is held responsible to see that all the material is covered. No longer can the "cop-out" be accepted, "Well, the children decided by the democratic process that we would not learn math this year."

Field Trips

Field trips, while not specifically limited, have been held to a minimum. No longer are children taken on trips twenty to thirty times a year. Field trips that have been taken related directly to material being studied in class. If the teacher is to cover the curriculum there just is not sufficient time to take them to movies, parks, or the other "fun" places to which parents can take them if they wish.

Homework

Homework, when assigned, is not "busy" work. There is no minimum or maximum amount of it. It is either supplemental to class work, such as corollary reading or reports, or it is classwork which was not finished in class. When given by the teacher it has a due date, and the teacher and pupils understand that the date is firm. Work done incorrectly or sloppily will be returned and must be redone until it is correct. This is an important area because we believe that neatness does count, that responsibility should be taught, and that the final exposure to any subject area must be a correct one.

Dress Code

The dress code is so vapid as to be virtually meaningless, except in one key respect: It is there and the parents agree to it. Thus, if a gross violation occurs, action can and will be taken. But it will not occur, because its mere inclusion in the handbook keeps out of the program those who feel that dirty clothes, dirty bodies, and bare feet anywhere are all right. And since it is an area where most, if not all, of the parents in the program have long felt a concern, the children come to school clean and neat and wearing shoes. Since they do, there is no peer pressure to have it any other way. Habit patterns of cleanliness and neatness need to be developed and reinforced at an early age. Unfortunately, plenty of pressure in the opposite direction will come in high school and college, but we will try to get our youngsters off to a good start in this area. And we have evidence in the form of a study done by one of the teachers in our high school district that a direct correlation exists between learning difficulties and a sloppy physical appearance and attitude.

Discipline

Discipline is not difficult to maintain. No children have been nailed to the desks, but in our first year the fourth-, fifth-, and sixth-grade children who had experienced several years of no discipline in other classrooms had some problems adjusting to the fact that they couldn't wander around the room or leave the room to go outside to play or talk back to the teacher whenever they felt like it. That comes as a shock to most new students even now. But the children have adjusted to it, and now even the new transferee feels peer pressure against that type of behavior and will not try it as much as he might have in another situation.

In instances where youngsters have gotten "out of line," particularly in talking back to the teacher or having an obvious "ho-hum" attitude, the parents are notified, the situation is explained to them, and an appropriate solution worked out. Behavior problems seldom arise now. Parents are comforted to know that if a problem appears they will be notified. Children are more reluctant to give full vent to their emotions if they know that their parents are going to hear about it from school.

Method of Instruction

For the most part, the classrooms are teacher directed and instructed. There is very little, if any, use of the contract method of self-instruction. The teacher teaches and the children learn. The children do a lot of work at the blackboard and in their seats and some in the library, but they are organized. No one wanders aimlessly around the room. Mastery of basic skills is heavily emphasized. Much of this mastery is learned by rote and, thus, there is much drill. It may not be new or innovative, but the youngsters do learn, and they are learning well. And they are now well ahead of most of their former classmates in their former schools. While we are not in a race with the rest of the district to see who can learn the most in the shortest time, our program is producing positive learning results at a good rate of speed. The fourth-grade class is well into long division, while our neighborhood school's fourth-grade class is learning the nines table in multiplication. There is drill in spelling and grammar. The first grade learns to read with both phonics and sight methods, but with the major emphasis on phonics, and with a continuity of method through the first three grades.

Report Cards

We still have not completely solved the problem of report cards. There is still resistance to giving a youngster an F. Perhaps we would be better off not to teach our youngsters to excel and to be producers. Perhaps we should let them just go back to the "regular district program." We may make them excel to the point where they will be frustrated bill payers for the rest of the future society in which they have to live. But that is another story.

Many teachers are really reluctant to give realistic grades. "An F will ruin the youngster's motivation. He will hate school and his teachers and will then quit trying." That is their rationale. We believe that is bunk. Children are people, and most people hate being told anything but the truth. Children know when they are being lied to or about. They know when they are not doing as well as the other children in the class. They can handle the truth, and their parents can too. The no-failure system has allowed many children in our district and elsewhere to be passed along for years from grade to grade doing poor to failing work until they reach a point where reality can no longer be ignored. Then the recognition of failure is a shock to everyone.

We do not want to penalize or to discourage the youngster who is doing work below average. We want to bring him up to par. However, we do him no service to let him and his parents think he is doing well when he is not. It may not be his fault if he is transferring in from another school, but he and his parents must be given the truth.

We have said to the teachers that if the youngster is doing failing work or work below grade level, and if in the opinion of the teacher a D or an F would truly destroy any motivation to improve, make an exception and give him a higher grade. But the parents must be informed of his exact status both actually and with relation to the rest of the class. The parents are given the results of the standardized testing twice a year so they can see the realities. Conferences are arranged with parents when children are not doing as well as the teacher thinks they should be. Every effort is made to insure a close working relationship between home and school to recognize and correct problems.

Successes of the Program

By this time the reader may have concluded one of the real truths of the A+ Program. A great deal of its success has been dependent on the quality and dedication of the teachers and principal selected to run it. They must be true professionals who know how to reach children but who refuse to grovel at their level. They must be intellectually honest enough to recognize their successes and weaknesses. They must have standards and value those standards and be gutsy enough to hold themselves and their students to those standards. And, unfortunately, they must be willing to do this against the terrific pressure and ridicule of members of their trade who are not professional and who have no standards and who resent those who have standards. For many teachers and principals there is nothing new in the A+ Program; it is "the way we've been operating for years." True enough, but where, as here, those methods have been under increasing fire, comfort may be received in the knowledge that those methods are appreciated by some of us.

Recently a parent related a conversation with her twelve-year-old son, who was not in the A+ Program. She was after him to get his homework done, to change into clean clothes, and to comb his hair before he went to school. His parting remark was, "Why do you care about it? They don't care at school!" Here was the core of the problem. For families who attempt to maintain standards, the failure of schools to back them is a source of anguish. A+ matches teachers and a program's standards to families with like standards.

Pressures Against the Program

The pressure against our teachers was mentioned above. We do not understand all of it. Some pressure is caused by the need of schools to avoid losing pupils, thus keeping A.D.A. money. But if some parents do not get a better program, they are going to go to the private and parochial schools anyway. The district has no idea how many parents have taken their children out now, but the private and parochial schools in the area are now nearly full and some have waiting lists, and district administration officials have admitted privately that more than 10 percent may have left already.

The pressure also occurs because we have provided an obvious answer to some of the failures of the "regular district program." Teachers and staff within that program are defensive. Some pressure occurs because some teachers genuinely believe that any standards or competition are psychologically bad for children. Some pressure occurs because these teachers say they do not want to be "labeled," but many of them have accepted the label of "open" teacher or "facilitator." Many of these who want no labels on them and noisily oppose "group labeling" are the same who are quick to label others as "Birchers," "conservatives," "radicals," and "cranks."

We are perfectly willing to have the A+ label removed if there is a tight guarantee that the program will remain totally intact. The difficulty is that without the label there is no way to identify it as an alternative to the "regular district program" without using such words as "structured" and "basics oriented," which leaves a dangerous implication on the other side. The administration has not answered this yet, because they are not ready to admit the lack of structure and basics orientation of the "regular district program." This is probably going to be a continuing problem until the district defines the "regular district program." Meanwhile, as long as teachers and parents understand the A+ Program and are willing to participate in it, we will get by.

In the area of selection of principals and teachers, we believe that this is neither our prerogative or responsibility. The function belongs to the administration, which is responsible to the board. It would greatly simplify our problems if we had the privilege, but it would further confuse the lines of authority and responsibility and would contribute to increasing the chaos in these areas within the district. Most of us are not willing to do that, even though the other two alternative programs in the district have been given the right. It has not been offered to us, but we should not exercise it if we have it.

CONCLUSIONS

Several conclusions may be drawn from our experience with the program.

First, if you contemplate starting such a program yourself, be prepared to devote the time to it to insure its success. It will not happen overnight. More than a hundred meetings of our group were held in 1973 alone. These involved two or more people and usually five or more. Most were at least two hours long, and all required several hours of preparation time.

It will help if you know clearly what you want to accomplish and what you do not want. You must also have a firm commitment that you will not take the easy way out and put your children in private schools, thus paying twice for their education. You must weed out of your group those who will quit as soon as their children receive a decent teacher this year and are not going to worry about next year until it gets here. You must do your "homework," being sure that the materials and information for any meeting are organized in advance. If alternative courses or solutions are possible, they must be thoroughly thought out in advance and the possible ramifications of each presented to the group for decision.

It will help if you have drafts of letters, proposals, plans, and so forth ready for each meeting. Hours can be wasted when the group tries to draft such material at a general meeting. One or two people can do it in advance and the total group can make modifications of the draft after the alternatives are explored. This method has the advantage of pointing the group in a direction and hastens the decision on the final wording.

Select as chairman or co-chairmen of your group those with a sincere conviction that your course is right who will stick with it no matter how thick the flak. As the pilots of 1944 found out, the flak gets thicker the closer you get to the enemy's heart. "Maintain a tight formation and radio silence," keep your group together, and do not let your opponents know your plans in advance. "Do not waste your bombs on a railroad spur when the locomotive works are only ten miles further on." Save your big fight for the board meeting where it counts instead of engaging in endless battles with individual teachers or principals. Some readers may object to my likening this to a war, but do not think for one minute that once you challenge the system you will not find yourself in a war. It may help you then to recognize that the axioms that win wars will help you be successful.

Second, divide your work and recruit people who can help with one task, but may not want to be an ongoing member of the group (or who may not be wanted). Many people have helped us prepare curriculum, check materials, make phone calls, and arrange car pools but are not ongoing members of the committee. They were available for a specific job, did it, and were finished. But they helped us tremendously.

Third, in setting up such a program your group needs to determine early what is the lower limit in your proposal that you will accept. You may make any proposal demands you want as long as you take a careful look at where you want to be when negotiations are finished and your program is in operation. It is a mistake to make your proposal so sweeping that you are dismissed as a "bunch of kooks." It is also a mistake to ask for too little. Before the program gets into operation there will be many changes, but if you know in advance the areas where you draw the line you can protect the integrity of the total package more carefully.

Fourth, today's educational picture has a positive need for sound, basic education in a structured environment for many children. They cannot learn, because of their individual make-up, in large, unstructured, and sometimes disorganized classes. Where those classes have come into vogue and have captured entire schools, learning problems have developed for children who need a structured program. Many teachers, too, work better in the structured environment. In the rush of educators to make school exciting and innovative, some have forgotten that some learning is occasionally difficult and is mastered only by hard work. Those things we treasure most are frequently those whose purchase came with the greatest sweat. Nothing is wrong with allowing children to learn this lesson also. Our program is successful because it meets the needs of pupils and parents with good results and the children are learning better and faster than they were before.

Fifth, keep the program out of politics and politics out of the program. Although our program grew out of the political arena, we have tried since its start to divorce the program from the politics of the members of the committee and the teachers. This is not always possible, the nature of people being what it is, but if we are to survive we must try. Fair-minded people see the need for both the open teaching methods and structured ones. The board members who defeated us have been very strong supporters in helping us. Two of them have their children in the open alternative program. Our fight has been against those who want only one method and would deny to everyone else the right to a differing preference. This type of person can be found anywhere, but in the education of our youngsters they are particularly dangerous. While demanding the right to their point of view, they deny that same right to their opponents when they gain control. This is hardly the example we want to set for our children.

Sixth, the program must be kept voluntary. Parents must put their children into it. It must not take over a whole neighborhood school so that local residents, if they do not want it, must take their children to another school. If possible it should have all six (or more) grades at one school. This means that it should be placed in schools that have at least two classes at each grade level. It needs to be in a school whose climate can permit divergent points of view without a fist fight. It needs to be placed in a school where a high percentage of the parents want it.

Finally, such programs may be the solution to keeping the public school system intact in America. School bond issues are failing across the country. Many middle-income families who bear the brunt of the financial burden for the public schools are rebelling against paying an increasing tax bill to support schools that turn out poorly prepared young people. Many do not like to see their values challenged by the schools and teachers they support. Many do not want untrained or partially trained amateurs, no matter what their good intentions, playing at psychiatry with their children's minds. They want the public schools to educate their children with a firm grounding in basic subjects and in those supplemental areas for which there is time to assist in development of reason and thought, to help instill responsibility and self-reliance based upon ability and knowledge, and to back the parents' desire for development of habit patterns to carry the youngster through life successfully.

Long ago the rich took most of their children out of the public schools for a variety of reasons, some good, many not so good. The poor have nowhere else they can afford to go. The middle-income group will stay or leave depending on the extent the system meets their differing needs and differing standards. Many have left already, and few of those will come back, but the struggle now will be to save the remainder. If they go, who will support the public schools? If they stay it will be because programs like Academics-Plus meet their needs without resort to private schools.

We have made our share of mistakes. Not everything has worked out as well as we might have hoped. But our overall average is very good despite some very determined opposition from some quarters and awful apathy from others. We are proud of our program. We believe it has value for children, parents, and teachers. For our own youngsters it may make the path of life a little straighter. Tomorrow's America can ill afford an uneducated, poorly prepared electorate. We hope our efforts will help to reverse the drift toward that dismal future for our country.